The Rise of Quantum Computing

Exploring the Next Frontier in Technology

Larry Adams

The Rise of Quantum Computing

TABLE OF CONTENTS

Chapter 1: Fundamental Concepts of Quantum Mechanics

Quantum Bits (Qubits)

Quantum computing represents a profound shift in how we process information, and at the core of this revolution lies the quantum bit, or qubit. Unlike classical bits, which are binary and can only exist in one of two states—0 or 1—qubits leverage the principles of quantum mechanics to exist in multiple states simultaneously, thanks to superposition. This unique property allows quantum computers to solve certain types of problems much more efficiently than classical computers.

A qubit can be visualized as a sphere, known as the Bloch sphere, where any point on the surface represents a possible state. The states $|0\rangle$ and $|1\rangle$ correspond to the north and south poles of this sphere, respectively. However, unlike a classical bit that would be strictly at one pole or the other, a qubit can exist anywhere on the surface of the sphere, representing a combination of both $|0\rangle$ and $|1\rangle$. This combination is described mathematically as a superposition of the basis states. The coefficients of this superposition are complex numbers, and their magnitudes squared must add up to 1, ensuring the total probability is conserved.

Entanglement is another cornerstone of qubit behavior. When qubits become entangled, the state of one qubit instantly influences the state of another, no matter the distance separating them. This phenomenon, famously referred to by Einstein as "spooky action at a distance," has been experimentally verified and is a key resource for many quantum algorithms. Entanglement allows for the creation of quantum states that cannot be described independently of each other, enabling more complex and correlated computations.

In practical terms, qubits can be realized in various physical systems. One common type is the superconducting qubit, which uses circuits made from superconducting materials cooled to extremely low temperatures. These circuits exhibit quantum behaviors and can be controlled using microwave pulses. Another type is the trapped ion qubit, where individual ions are held in place using electromagnetic fields and manipulated with laser beams. Photonic qubits, which use the quantum states of photons, offer another approach, particularly appealing for quantum communication due to their ability to travel long distances without significant loss.

Quantum gates are the building blocks of quantum circuits, analogous to classical logic gates but with the capability to manipulate qubits in superposition and entangled states. Common gates include the Pauli gates (X, Y, Z), the Hadamard gate (H), and the CNOT gate, which entangles two qubits. The Hadamard gate, for example, creates a superposition state from a classical bit, while the CNOT gate flips the state of a target qubit conditional on the state of a control qubit, enabling entanglement.

Measurement in quantum mechanics collapses a qubit's superposition into one of the basis states, 0 or 1, with probabilities determined by the amplitudes of the superposition. This collapse is probabilistic and inherently disrupts the quantum state, a challenge for quantum computing known as decoherence. Decoherence occurs when a qubit interacts with its environment, causing the loss of quantum information. To mitigate this, qubits are often isolated from external disturbances, and error correction codes are employed to detect and correct errors without measuring the qubits directly.

The differences between quantum and classical mechanics underscore the transformative potential of quantum computing. Classical bits operate deterministically, with each computation step following logically from the previous one. In contrast, quantum computation leverages the probabilistic nature of quantum mechanics, enabling simultaneous exploration of multiple solutions. This parallelism is what grants quantum computers their potential advantage for certain problems, such as factoring large numbers or simulating quantum systems.

Quantum algorithms are designed to harness the unique properties of qubits. Shor's algorithm, for instance, can factorize integers exponentially faster than the best-known classical algorithms, posing a significant threat to current cryptographic systems. Grover's algorithm, on the other hand, provides a quadratic speedup for unstructured search problems. These algorithms illustrate the profound implications of qubits for computational tasks that are intractable for classical computers.

Despite their promise, qubits face significant challenges. Maintaining quantum coherence is difficult, as qubits are highly sensitive to their environment. Any interaction with external particles or fields can lead to decoherence, effectively destroying the quantum information. Researchers are actively developing techniques to extend coherence times and improve qubit isolation. Superconducting qubits, for example, are kept at temperatures close to absolute zero to minimize thermal noise, while trapped ion qubits are isolated in ultra-high vacuum chambers.

Quantum error correction is another critical area of research. Unlike classical error correction, which deals with discrete bit flips or signal loss, quantum error correction must account for continuous errors arising from decoherence and other quantum-specific phenomena. Techniques such as the surface code and the Bacon-Shor code are being developed to protect quantum information. These methods involve encoding logical qubits into entangled states of multiple physical qubits, allowing errors to be detected and corrected without directly measuring the qubits.

The hardware architectures supporting qubits are diverse and continually evolving. Superconducting qubits, developed by companies like IBM and Google, have shown significant progress, with Google achieving quantum supremacy in 2019 by performing a specific task faster than the best-known classical algorithm. Trapped ion systems, pursued by companies like IonQ, offer high-fidelity qubit operations and long coherence times. Photonic qubits, meanwhile, hold promise for scalable quantum networks, as demonstrated by research in quantum communication and cryptography.

Looking ahead, hybrid approaches combining different types of qubits and leveraging their respective strengths are being explored. For instance, integrating superconducting qubits with photonic links could enable long-distance quantum communication while maintaining fast, reliable computation. Similarly, combining trapped ion qubits with superconducting circuits might offer new pathways for scalable quantum processors.

In conclusion, qubits are the fundamental units of quantum information, embodying the principles of superposition and entanglement that differentiate quantum computing from classical computing. Their unique properties enable powerful quantum algorithms and applications, pushing the boundaries of what is computationally possible. However, realizing the full potential of qubits requires overcoming significant technical challenges, particularly in maintaining coherence and developing robust error correction. As research and development continue, the field of quantum computing is poised to revolutionize technology, science, and beyond, driven by the extraordinary capabilities of qubits.

Superposition and Entanglement

Superposition and entanglement lie at the heart of quantum mechanics, offering a glimpse into the strange and counterintuitive nature of the quantum world. These principles are not just theoretical curiosities; they are the foundations upon which quantum computing is built. Understanding them is crucial to grasping how quantum computers can perform tasks that are impossible for classical computers.

Superposition is a fundamental concept in quantum mechanics that allows particles, such as electrons or photons, to exist in multiple states simultaneously. A classical bit, the basic unit of information in classical computing, can be either 0 or 1. In contrast, a quantum bit, or qubit, can be in a state that is a mixture of 0 and 1. This mixture is known as a superposition. Mathematically, it is represented as a linear combination of the basis states $|0\rangle$ and $|1\rangle$. The coefficients of this combination are complex numbers, and their magnitudes squared give the probabilities of measuring the qubit in each state. This probabilistic nature is a hallmark of quantum mechanics.

To visualize superposition, imagine a spinning coin. While spinning, the coin is in a superposition of heads and tails. It is only when the coin lands that it shows one definite face. Similarly, a qubit in superposition is in an indeterminate state until it is measured. Upon measurement, the superposition collapses to one of the basis states, either 0 or 1, with probabilities determined by the superposition's coefficients. This collapse is a purely quantum phenomenon with no classical counterpart.

Entanglement is another quintessential quantum property, where the states of two or more particles become intertwined such that the state of one particle cannot be described independently of the state of the other(s). When particles are entangled, the measurement of one particle's state instantly determines the state of the other, regardless of the distance separating them. This non-local connection defies classical intuition and has been experimentally verified through numerous tests of Bell's inequalities.

Consider a pair of entangled qubits. If one qubit is measured and found to be in the state $|0\rangle$, the other qubit, no matter how far away, will immediately be found in the state $|1\rangle$ if they were prepared in a specific entangled state. This instant correlation occurs even if the qubits are light-years apart, a phenomenon that perplexed even Einstein, who famously referred to it as "spooky action at a distance." The power of entanglement is harnessed in various quantum technologies, including quantum cryptography and quantum teleportation.

In the realm of quantum computing, superposition and entanglement enable the execution of complex computations more efficiently than classical computers. Superposition allows quantum computers to explore many possible solutions simultaneously. For instance, while a classical computer would need to evaluate each possible solution one by one, a quantum computer can process a vast number of possibilities at the same time. This parallelism is a significant advantage for certain types of problems, such as factoring large numbers or searching unsorted databases.

Entanglement further enhances this computational power by allowing qubits to be correlated in ways that classical bits cannot. Quantum algorithms like Shor's algorithm for factoring and Grover's search algorithm exploit entanglement to perform tasks exponentially faster than the best-known classical algorithms. In Shor's algorithm, for example, entangled qubits are used to find the period of a function, a key step in the factoring process. Grover's algorithm, on the other hand, uses entanglement to search an unsorted database in quadratic time, significantly faster than any classical approach.

The practical implementation of superposition and entanglement requires precise control over qubits and their interactions. Various physical systems have been developed to create and manipulate qubits, each with its own advantages and challenges. Superconducting circuits, trapped ions, and photonic systems are among the leading technologies. Superconducting qubits, used by companies like IBM and Google, are manipulated using microwave pulses to create and control superposition states. Trapped ion qubits, held in place by electromagnetic fields, are manipulated with laser beams to achieve superposition and entanglement. Photonic qubits, which use the polarization states of photons, are particularly useful for quantum communication due to their ability to travel long distances without significant loss.

Maintaining superposition and entanglement in qubits is a delicate task. Qubits are highly sensitive to their environment, and any interaction with external particles or fields can cause decoherence, leading to the loss of quantum information. Decoherence is one of the biggest challenges in building practical quantum computers. To mitigate this, qubits are often isolated in ultra-cold environments, and error correction techniques are employed. Quantum error correction involves encoding a logical qubit into a highly entangled state of multiple physical qubits, allowing for the detection and correction of errors without directly measuring the qubits.

Despite these challenges, significant progress has been made in creating stable qubits with long coherence times. Researchers are continually developing new materials and technologies to improve the fidelity of quantum operations. For example, advances in superconducting materials have led to qubits with longer coherence times and higher gate fidelities. Similarly, improvements in laser and trapping technologies have enhanced the performance of trapped ion qubits.

The implications of superposition and entanglement extend beyond computing. In quantum communication, entanglement is used to create secure communication channels through quantum key distribution (QKD). QKD allows two parties to share a secret key, which can be used to encrypt and decrypt messages, with the security guaranteed by the principles of quantum mechanics. Any attempt to eavesdrop on the communication will disturb the entangled states, alerting the parties to the presence of an intruder. This level of security is unattainable with classical cryptographic methods.

Quantum teleportation is another fascinating application of entanglement. It involves transferring the state of a qubit from one location to another without physically moving the qubit itself. This is achieved by entangling a pair of qubits, one at the sender's location and one at the receiver's. The sender then performs a measurement on their qubit and the qubit to be teleported, sending the result to the receiver. Using this information, the receiver can reconstruct the original state on their qubit. This process, while not teleportation in the traditional science fiction sense, demonstrates the power of entanglement in transmitting quantum information.

In conclusion, superposition and entanglement are the bedrock principles of quantum mechanics that enable the extraordinary capabilities of quantum computing. They allow qubits to exist in multiple states simultaneously and to be correlated in ways that classical bits cannot. These properties open up new possibilities for computation, communication, and beyond, offering solutions to problems that are currently intractable with classical technology. As research and development continue, the potential applications of superposition and entanglement will undoubtedly expand, driving further innovation and discovery in the quantum realm.

Quantum Gates and Circuits

Quantum gates and circuits form the backbone of quantum computing, akin to classical logic gates and circuits in traditional computing. These elements manipulate qubits, enabling the execution of quantum algorithms that can outperform their classical counterparts. To appreciate the power and complexity of quantum gates and circuits, one must delve into their principles, types, and applications.

A quantum gate is a basic quantum circuit operating on a small number of qubits. Quantum gates are reversible, unlike most classical logic gates. This reversibility is a result of quantum mechanics, where the evolution of a closed system is unitary. Each quantum gate is represented by a unitary matrix, which transforms the state of the qubits it acts upon. The simplest quantum gate is the Pauli-X gate, analogous to the classical NOT gate. It flips the state of a single qubit: if the qubit is in state $|0\rangle$, the X gate transforms it to $|1\rangle$, and vice versa.

Another fundamental gate is the Hadamard gate, which creates superposition. When applied to a qubit in the state $|0\rangle$, the Hadamard gate transforms it into an equal superposition of $|0\rangle$ and $|1\rangle$. Mathematically, this superposition is represented as $(|0\rangle + |1\rangle)/\sqrt{2}$. The Hadamard gate is crucial for many quantum algorithms, as it allows for the exploration of multiple states simultaneously.

Controlled gates, such as the Controlled-NOT (CNOT) gate, operate on two qubits. The CNOT gate flips the state of the second qubit (the target) if the first qubit (the control) is in the state $|1\rangle$. The CNOT gate is essential for creating entangled states, which are vital for quantum computations. For example, applying a Hadamard gate to the control qubit followed by a CNOT gate can create a Bell state, an entangled state of two qubits.

In addition to these basic gates, there are more complex gates like the Pauli-Y and Pauli-Z gates, which apply specific phase changes to qubits. The phase shift gates, such as the S and T gates, are also important. The S gate applies a $\pi/2$ phase shift, while the T gate applies a $\pi/4$ phase shift. These gates are essential for constructing more complex quantum circuits and for implementing quantum algorithms like Shor's algorithm for factoring large numbers.

Quantum circuits are networks of quantum gates arranged to perform a specific computation. A quantum circuit begins with qubits in a defined initial state, typically $|0\rangle$, and ends with a measurement that collapses the qubits into classical bits. The arrangement and combination of quantum gates within the circuit determine the computation's outcome.

Designing a quantum circuit involves several steps. First, the problem must be translated into a quantum algorithm. This process often requires rethinking the problem in terms of quantum mechanics, leveraging superposition and entanglement. Next, the algorithm is mapped onto a sequence of quantum gates. This step can be challenging, as it requires optimizing the circuit to minimize errors and decoherence, which are significant issues in current quantum hardware.

One of the simplest quantum algorithms is the Deutsch-Jozsa algorithm, which determines whether a given function is constant or balanced. The algorithm uses a single evaluation of the function, showcasing the power of quantum computing. The circuit for the Deutsch-Jozsa algorithm uses Hadamard gates to create superposition and a function evaluation gate to encode the function's properties into the qubits. The final Hadamard gates and measurement reveal the function's nature.

Another notable quantum algorithm is Grover's search algorithm, which finds a marked item in an unsorted database quadratically faster than any classical algorithm. Grover's algorithm involves iterating a quantum circuit called the Grover operator, which amplifies the probability of the marked item's state. The circuit uses Hadamard gates, Oracle gates that mark the item, and diffusion operators that enhance the marked state's amplitude. The power of Grover's algorithm lies in its ability to leverage quantum parallelism and interference to achieve a significant speedup.

Quantum circuits can also implement more complex algorithms, such as Shor's algorithm for factoring large numbers. Shor's algorithm relies on the quantum Fourier transform (QFT), a quantum analog of the classical discrete Fourier transform. The QFT is implemented using a sequence of Hadamard gates and controlled phase shift gates. Shor's algorithm demonstrates the potential of quantum computing to solve problems that are intractable for classical computers, posing a threat to classical cryptographic systems based on the difficulty of factoring.

Building practical quantum circuits requires addressing several challenges. Quantum gates must be implemented with high fidelity to minimize errors. Current quantum hardware, such as superconducting qubits and trapped ions, is prone to errors due to interactions with the environment and imperfections in gate operations. Error correction techniques are crucial for mitigating these errors. Quantum error correction involves encoding logical qubits into entangled states of multiple physical qubits, allowing for the detection and correction of errors without directly measuring the qubits.

The surface code is a leading quantum error correction code that uses a 2D lattice of qubits with nearest-neighbor interactions. It can detect and correct both bit-flip and phase-flip errors, providing a robust foundation for fault-tolerant quantum computing. Implementing the surface code requires a large number of physical qubits and precise control over their interactions, posing significant engineering challenges.

Despite these challenges, significant progress has been made in building practical quantum circuits. Advances in quantum hardware, such as longer coherence times and higher gate fidelities, have enabled the implementation of more complex quantum algorithms. Quantum processors with dozens of qubits are now available, allowing for the exploration of quantum algorithms and applications in various fields, from cryptography to materials science.

In addition to hardware improvements, software tools for designing and simulating quantum circuits have advanced. Quantum programming languages like Qiskit, Cirq, and Quipper provide high-level abstractions for constructing and optimizing quantum circuits. These tools allow researchers and developers to experiment with quantum algorithms and test their implementations on real quantum hardware.

The potential applications of quantum circuits extend beyond computing. Quantum simulations, which use quantum circuits to model quantum systems, can provide insights into chemistry, materials science, and fundamental physics. Quantum communication, leveraging quantum circuits for secure communication protocols, promises unbreakable cryptographic systems. Quantum metrology, using quantum circuits for high-precision measurements, can enhance the sensitivity of sensors and improve timekeeping.

Quantum gates and circuits are the building blocks of quantum computing, enabling the execution of quantum algorithms that harness the unique properties of qubits. From basic gates like the Hadamard and CNOT gates to complex circuits implementing algorithms like Grover's and Shor's, these elements are central to the quantum revolution. As research and development continue, the capabilities of quantum circuits will expand, unlocking new possibilities for computation, communication, and beyond.

Measurement and Decoherence

Measurement and decoherence are pivotal concepts in quantum mechanics, deeply influencing the operation and reliability of quantum computers. Understanding the interplay between these phenomena is essential for anyone venturing into the realm of quantum computing, as they pose both challenges and opportunities in harnessing the full potential of quantum technology.

Measurement in quantum computing is fundamentally different from classical measurement. When we measure a quantum system, we collapse its wave function from a superposition of states into a single state. This process is probabilistic, governed by the Born rule, which states that the probability of collapsing into a particular state is proportional to the square of the amplitude of that state's wave function. For instance, if a qubit is in a superposition of $|0\rangle$ and $|1\rangle$ with equal probability amplitudes, measuring it will yield either $|0\rangle$ or $|1\rangle$ with a 50% probability for each.

To illustrate, consider a qubit in the state $(|0\rangle + |1\rangle)/\sqrt{2}$. This superposition means the qubit has an equal chance of being found in either the $|0\rangle$ or $|1\rangle$ state upon measurement.

However, once the measurement is made, the qubit's state collapses into one of these definite states, and the superposition is lost. This collapse is a direct consequence of the measurement process and is a key feature distinguishing quantum mechanics from classical physics.

The act of measuring a quantum system introduces a level of uncertainty and randomness that can be both a resource and a hindrance. On the one hand, it enables the unique capabilities of quantum computers, such as solving certain problems exponentially faster than classical computers. On the other hand, it complicates the task of extracting reliable information from quantum computations, as the process of measurement inherently disrupts the quantum state.

Decoherence is another critical concept closely related to measurement. It refers to the loss of coherence in a quantum system due to its interaction with the environment. When a quantum system interacts with its surroundings, it can no longer maintain superposition and entanglement, which are essential for quantum computation. Decoherence effectively causes a quantum system to behave more classically, undermining the advantages offered by quantum mechanics.

Imagine a qubit isolated in a perfect vacuum, undisturbed by its environment. This qubit can maintain its quantum properties indefinitely, allowing it to perform quantum computations. However, in reality, qubits are susceptible to various sources of noise and interference, such as electromagnetic radiation, thermal fluctuations, and material defects. These interactions cause the qubit to lose its coherence, leading to errors in quantum computations.

The timescale over which a qubit maintains its coherence is known as the coherence time. For practical quantum computing, it is crucial to perform computations within this coherence time to minimize errors. Researchers are continually working to extend coherence times through improved qubit designs, error correction techniques, and environmental shielding.

Decoherence poses a significant challenge for quantum computing, but it also provides a profound insight into the transition from quantum to classical behavior. By studying decoherence, scientists gain a deeper understanding of how classical physics emerges from quantum mechanics. This knowledge is not only fundamental to the philosophy of physics but also practical for developing strategies to mitigate decoherence in quantum systems.

One approach to combat decoherence is quantum error correction. Unlike classical error correction, which typically involves redundancy and majority voting, quantum error correction relies on encoding logical qubits into entangled states of multiple physical qubits. This encoding allows for the detection and correction of errors without directly measuring the qubits, thereby preserving their quantum properties.

A widely researched quantum error correction code is the surface code, which arranges qubits in a two-dimensional lattice. The surface code can correct both bit-flip and phase-flip errors, providing a robust framework for fault-tolerant quantum computing. Implementing the surface code requires precise control over qubit interactions and the ability to perform multiple rounds of error detection and correction within the coherence time.

Another strategy to mitigate decoherence involves isolating qubits from their environment as much as possible. This can be achieved through techniques such as cryogenic cooling, which reduces thermal noise, and the use of materials with low defects and impurities. Superconducting qubits, trapped ions, and topological qubits are among the leading qubit technologies that offer promising coherence times and are actively being developed by researchers.

The impact of decoherence is not limited to quantum computing. It also affects quantum communication and quantum cryptography, where maintaining the coherence of quantum states is essential for secure information transfer. Quantum key distribution (QKD), for example, relies on the principles of quantum mechanics to ensure the security of cryptographic keys. Decoherence can compromise the security of QKD by introducing errors and reducing the fidelity of the transmitted quantum states.

To address these challenges, researchers are exploring various methods to enhance the robustness of quantum communication systems. One approach is the use of quantum repeaters, which extend the range of quantum communication by correcting errors and amplifying signals without measuring the quantum states. Quantum repeaters leverage entanglement swapping and quantum error correction to maintain the integrity of quantum information over long distances.

Decoherence also plays a crucial role in quantum simulations, where quantum computers are used to model complex quantum systems. Accurate quantum simulations require maintaining coherence over the duration of the simulation to capture the true behavior of the system being studied.

Decoherence can introduce inaccuracies and limit the ability of quantum simulations to provide meaningful insights into phenomena such as high-temperature superconductivity, chemical reactions, and fundamental particle interactions.

Despite the challenges posed by measurement and decoherence, the field of quantum computing continues to advance rapidly. Researchers are making significant progress in developing techniques to mitigate decoherence, improve qubit coherence times, and design fault-tolerant quantum systems. These advancements bring us closer to realizing the full potential of quantum computing and unlocking new possibilities in computation, communication, and beyond.

Measurement and decoherence are intertwined aspects of quantum mechanics that profoundly impact the operation and reliability of quantum computers. Understanding these phenomena is essential for developing practical quantum technologies and harnessing the unique capabilities of quantum systems. As research progresses, the strategies to manage and mitigate the effects of measurement and decoherence will continue to evolve, paving the way for more robust and powerful quantum devices.

Key Differences from Classical Mechanics

Classical mechanics and quantum mechanics, while both fundamental to our understanding of the physical world, operate on vastly different principles and scales. The stark contrasts between these two realms of physics not only highlight the unique behaviors of microscopic systems but also underscore the limitations of classical mechanics in describing phenomena at the quantum level. Grasping these key differences is crucial for anyone delving into the intricacies of quantum mechanics.

Classical mechanics, originating from the work of Newton, describes the motion of macroscopic objects using deterministic laws. Objects in classical mechanics have well-defined positions and velocities, and their future behavior can be precisely predicted if their current state is known. For example, if you know the initial position and velocity of a baseball, you can accurately calculate its trajectory and where it will land. This predictability is a hallmark of classical physics, where the state of a system at one point in time determines its state at any future time.

In contrast, quantum mechanics introduces a level of fundamental uncertainty. At the quantum scale, particles such as electrons do not have definite positions and velocities until they are measured. Instead, they are described by wave functions, which provide probabilities for finding a particle in a particular state. This intrinsic uncertainty is encapsulated in Heisenberg's uncertainty principle, which states that it is impossible to simultaneously know both the exact position and momentum of a particle. This principle challenges our classical intuition and reshapes our understanding of the nature of reality.

Consider the famous double-slit experiment, which vividly illustrates the probabilistic nature of quantum mechanics. When electrons are fired at a barrier with two slits, they create an interference pattern on a detector screen, a pattern that is characteristic of waves. However, if one attempts to measure which slit each electron passes through, the interference pattern disappears, and the electrons behave like particles. This experiment reveals the dual wave-particle nature of quantum objects and shows how measurement affects the state of a quantum system.

Another fundamental difference lies in the concept of superposition. In classical mechanics, an object can be in only one state at a time. A coin, for instance, can be either heads or tails, but not both simultaneously. Quantum mechanics, however, allows particles to exist in multiple states at once, a phenomenon known as superposition. A qubit, the basic unit of information in quantum computing, can be in a superposition of the $|0\rangle$ and $|1\rangle$ states, enabling quantum computers to perform many calculations simultaneously. This capability is what gives quantum computers their potential to solve certain problems much faster than classical computers.

Entanglement is another striking feature of quantum mechanics with no classical counterpart. When particles become entangled, their states are correlated in such a way that the state of one particle instantly determines the state of the other, regardless of the distance separating them. This phenomenon puzzled even Einstein, who referred to it as "spooky action at a distance." Entanglement has profound implications for quantum communication and computing, enabling protocols like quantum teleportation and superdense coding. The non-locality of entanglement challenges the classical notion of locality, where objects are only directly influenced by their immediate surroundings.

The concept of measurement in quantum mechanics also diverges significantly from classical mechanics. In the classical world, measurement merely reveals a pre-existing property without altering the state of the system. However, in quantum mechanics, measurement plays an active role in determining the outcome. When a quantum system is measured, its wave function collapses to a single eigenstate, a process that is inherently probabilistic. This collapse mechanism introduces a level of randomness that is absent in classical measurements, where outcomes are entirely deterministic.

Quantum tunneling is yet another phenomenon that defies classical expectations. In classical mechanics, an object needs sufficient energy to overcome a potential barrier. A ball, for instance, must have enough kinetic energy to roll over a hill. Quantum mechanics, however, allows particles to tunnel through barriers even if they do not possess the requisite energy. This tunneling effect is crucial in many physical processes, such as nuclear fusion in stars and the operation of tunnel diodes in electronics. It highlights the non-intuitive nature of quantum mechanics, where particles can traverse classically forbidden regions.

The mathematical frameworks of classical and quantum mechanics also differ fundamentally. Classical mechanics relies on Newton's laws of motion, expressed through differential equations that describe the trajectories of objects. Quantum mechanics, on the other hand, uses the Schrödinger equation to describe the evolution of wave functions over time. The solutions to the Schrödinger equation are wave functions, which encode the probabilities of finding particles in various states. This shift from deterministic trajectories to probabilistic wave functions marks a profound departure from classical thinking.

In addition to wave functions, quantum mechanics employs operators to represent physical observables such as position, momentum, and energy. These operators act on wave functions to extract information about the system. For example, the Hamiltonian operator corresponds to the total energy of the system and plays a central role in determining the time evolution of the wave function. The use of operators and wave functions introduces a level of abstraction that is absent in classical mechanics, where physical quantities are directly measurable and do not require such mathematical constructs.

The realms of application for classical and quantum mechanics also differ significantly. Classical mechanics excels in describing the behavior of macroscopic objects, from the motion of planets to the dynamics of vehicles. Its principles are intuitive and align with everyday experiences. Quantum mechanics, however, is essential for understanding the behavior of microscopic particles, such as electrons, atoms, and molecules. It provides the foundation for modern technologies like semiconductors, lasers, and MRI machines. The necessity of quantum mechanics becomes evident in domains where classical mechanics fails to accurately describe observed phenomena.

The transition from classical to quantum mechanics is not just a shift in mathematical formalism but a profound change in our conceptual understanding of the physical world. It challenges our intuitions about determinism, locality, and the nature of reality itself. Embracing the counterintuitive aspects of quantum mechanics opens the door to new technologies and deeper insights into the fabric of the universe.

Despite their differences, classical and quantum mechanics are not mutually exclusive. Classical mechanics emerges as an approximation of quantum mechanics in the macroscopic limit, where the effects of quantum uncertainty and superposition become negligible. This correspondence principle ensures that the well-established laws of classical physics are consistent with the more fundamental principles of quantum mechanics in appropriate regimes. It highlights the continuity of scientific theories, where new theories build upon and refine the framework established by their predecessors.

Understanding the key differences between classical and quantum mechanics is essential for navigating the complex landscape of modern physics. These differences not only illuminate the unique behaviors of quantum systems but also underscore the limitations of classical mechanics in describing the microscopic world. By appreciating these distinctions, one gains a deeper insight into the nature of reality and the remarkable phenomena that lie at the heart of quantum mechanics.

Chapter 2: Building Blocks of Quantum Computers

Types of Qubits: Photonic, Superconducting, Trapped Ions

Photonic, superconducting, and trapped ion qubits each offer distinct advantages and challenges, representing the forefront of quantum computing technology. Understanding these types of qubits is essential for navigating the rapidly evolving landscape of quantum hardware and appreciating the unique contributions each makes to the field.

Photonic qubits leverage the properties of light particles, or photons, to encode and process quantum information. Photons are particularly advantageous because they are naturally resistant to decoherence, a phenomenon where quantum information is lost due to interactions with the environment. This robustness makes photonic qubits ideal for quantum communication, enabling the transmission of quantum information over long distances with minimal loss. Furthermore, photons can be manipulated using well-established optical components like beam splitters, mirrors, and waveguides, making them a versatile choice for quantum experiments.

One of the primary methods for creating photonic qubits involves using polarization states of photons. A photon polarized in the horizontal direction can represent the $|0\rangle$ state, while a photon polarized in the vertical direction represents the $|1\rangle$ state. Superpositions of these states can be achieved using polarization beam splitters and wave plates, allowing for the full range of quantum operations. Photonic qubits can also be created using path encoding, where the photon's presence in one of two possible paths represents the logical states.

The development of photonic quantum computers has led to significant advancements in integrated photonics, where optical components are miniaturized and integrated onto a single chip. This approach promises scalability and integration with existing semiconductor technologies, potentially leading to practical and compact quantum devices. However, challenges remain, particularly in the generation and detection of single photons with high efficiency and the implementation of two-photon quantum gates, which are essential for universal quantum computing.

Superconducting qubits, on the other hand, harness the principles of superconductivity to create quantum bits. These qubits are typically constructed using superconducting circuits that can carry electrical currents without resistance when cooled to cryogenic temperatures. The most common type of superconducting qubit is the transmon qubit, which is designed to reduce sensitivity to charge noise, thereby enhancing coherence times.

A transmon qubit consists of a superconducting island connected to a larger circuit via a Josephson junction, a non-linear inductor that allows for the creation of discrete energy levels. The quantum states $|0\rangle$ and $|1\rangle$ correspond to the ground and first excited states of the circuit, and quantum operations are performed using microwave pulses to induce transitions between these states. The scalability of superconducting qubits is one of their main advantages, as they can be fabricated using standard semiconductor processes and integrated into large-scale quantum processors.

Despite their promise, superconducting qubits face challenges related to coherence times and error rates. Decoherence arises from interactions with the surrounding environment, including stray electromagnetic fields and material impurities. Researchers are continually working to mitigate these effects by improving the design and fabrication of qubits, developing error-correcting codes, and enhancing cryogenic systems. Superconducting qubits are currently among the most advanced in terms of practical quantum computation, with several companies and research institutions developing quantum processors based on this technology.

Trapped ion qubits offer another compelling approach to quantum computing. These qubits are created by trapping individual ions, typically atoms with a single electron removed, using electromagnetic fields. The trapped ions are then manipulated using laser pulses to perform quantum operations. The internal electronic states of the ions serve as the qubit states, with the ground state representing $|0\rangle$ and an excited state representing $|1\rangle$.

One of the significant advantages of trapped ion qubits is their excellent coherence properties. Ions can be isolated from their environment with high precision, reducing the effects of decoherence. Additionally, trapped ion systems allow for high-fidelity quantum gates, where interactions between ions can be precisely controlled using laser pulses. This level of control enables the implementation of complex quantum algorithms with relatively low error rates.

The scalability of trapped ion quantum computers is a topic of ongoing research. While current systems can reliably trap and manipulate tens of ions, scaling up to hundreds or thousands of qubits presents significant technical challenges. One approach to addressing this issue involves developing modular architectures, where multiple smaller ion traps are interconnected to form a larger quantum processor. This modular approach could enable the construction of more extensive and more powerful quantum computers.

Each type of qubit—photonic, superconducting, and trapped ion—brings unique strengths and faces specific challenges. Photonic qubits excel in quantum communication and integration with optical technologies, making them ideal for applications where long-distance transmission of quantum information is crucial. Superconducting qubits offer the advantage of scalability and integration with existing semiconductor fabrication techniques, positioning them as a leading candidate for building large-scale quantum processors. Trapped ion qubits stand out for their coherence properties and precision control, making them suitable for high-fidelity quantum operations and error correction.

The choice of qubit technology depends on the specific requirements of the quantum application in question. For instance, quantum communication networks may favor photonic qubits due to their robustness in transmission, while quantum computing tasks that require large numbers of qubits might lean towards superconducting or trapped ion qubits. Researchers and engineers must carefully consider these factors when designing and building quantum systems, balancing the trade-offs between coherence, scalability, and operational fidelity.

As the field of quantum computing continues to advance, hybrid approaches that combine different types of qubits may emerge, leveraging the strengths of each to overcome their individual limitations. For example, a quantum computer could use superconducting qubits for processing and photonic qubits for communication, creating a versatile and powerful system. Such hybrid architectures hold the promise of unlocking new capabilities and accelerating the realization of practical quantum technologies.

In summary, the exploration of photonic, superconducting, and trapped ion qubits reveals the diverse and innovative approaches being pursued in the quest for quantum computing. Each type of qubit offers unique advantages and faces distinct challenges, reflecting the complexity and richness of the field. By understanding these different qubit technologies, one gains a deeper appreciation for the current state of quantum computing and the exciting possibilities that lie ahead. The ongoing research and development in this area promise to bring transformative advancements, paving the way for a new era of computational power and technological innovation.

Quantum Hardware and Architectures

Quantum hardware and architectures are the backbone of the burgeoning field of quantum computing. They provide the physical foundation upon which quantum algorithms are executed, and they dictate the performance, scalability, and practical applications of quantum computers. The evolution of quantum hardware is driven by the quest to create stable, scalable, and efficient quantum systems, capable of solving complex problems beyond the reach of classical computers.

Quantum hardware can be broadly categorized into several types based on the underlying technology used to create qubits, the basic units of quantum information. These technologies include superconducting circuits, trapped ions, photonics, and topological qubits, among others. Each technology offers unique advantages and faces specific challenges, influencing the design and capabilities of quantum architectures.

Superconducting circuits are one of the most advanced and widely researched types of quantum hardware. These circuits operate at cryogenic temperatures, where certain materials exhibit zero electrical resistance, allowing for the creation of stable and coherent qubits. Superconducting qubits, such as transmons, are manipulated using microwave pulses to perform quantum operations. The scalability of superconducting qubits is a significant advantage, as they can be fabricated using techniques similar to those used in classical semiconductor manufacturing. However, maintaining the delicate quantum states in a noisy environment remains a challenge, necessitating sophisticated error correction protocols.

Trapped ions represent another promising approach to quantum hardware. In this technology, individual ions are confined and manipulated using electromagnetic fields. The internal states of the ions serve as qubits, which can be precisely controlled with laser pulses. Trapped ion systems are known for their exceptional coherence times and high-fidelity quantum gates. These properties make them ideal for implementing intricate quantum algorithms. However, scaling up trapped ion systems to accommodate a large number of qubits is a complex task, requiring advances in ion trap design and control.

Photonic quantum computers utilize light particles, or photons, to encode and process quantum information. Photons are inherently resistant to decoherence, making them suitable for long-distance quantum communication. Photonic qubits can be manipulated using optical components such as beam splitters and waveguides. Integrated photonics, where optical elements are fabricated on a single chip, offers a path toward scalable quantum systems. Nevertheless, challenges in generating and detecting single photons with high efficiency must be addressed to realize practical photonic quantum computers.

Topological qubits, a more theoretical approach, promise robust protection against decoherence through the use of exotic states of matter known as anyons. These qubits leverage the mathematical properties of topological phases to encode information in a way that is inherently resistant to local disturbances. While the practical realization of topological qubits is still in its infancy, they hold the potential to revolutionize quantum computing by significantly reducing error rates.

The architecture of a quantum computer encompasses not only the qubits themselves but also the interconnects, control systems, and error correction mechanisms that enable the execution of quantum algorithms. Quantum architectures must address several critical challenges to be viable for practical applications. These include qubit coherence, gate fidelity, qubit connectivity, and error correction.

Qubit coherence refers to the duration over which a qubit can maintain its quantum state without being corrupted by environmental interactions. High coherence times are essential for performing complex quantum computations. Researchers are continually developing new materials and techniques to enhance qubit coherence, such as surface passivation and improved cryogenic environments.

Gate fidelity measures the accuracy with which quantum operations are performed. High-fidelity gates are crucial for implementing reliable quantum algorithms. Imperfect gates introduce errors that can accumulate and degrade the performance of a quantum computer. Techniques such as pulse shaping and optimized control sequences are employed to maximize gate fidelity.

Qubit connectivity, or the ability to establish interactions between qubits, is another vital aspect of quantum architecture. In many quantum algorithms, qubits need to interact with one another to perform entangling operations. Different quantum technologies offer varying degrees of qubit connectivity. For instance, superconducting qubits can be coupled using microwave resonators, while trapped ions can interact through collective vibrational modes. Efficient qubit connectivity enables the implementation of complex quantum circuits with fewer resources.

Error correction is perhaps the most significant challenge in quantum computing. Quantum error correction involves encoding logical qubits into multiple physical qubits to detect and correct errors that occur during computation. This process requires sophisticated algorithms and additional qubits, increasing the overhead for practical quantum systems. Surface codes and topological codes are among the leading error correction schemes being explored. These codes are designed to detect and correct both bit-flip and phase-flip errors, ensuring the stability of quantum information over extended periods.

Quantum architectures must also consider the integration of classical control systems. Quantum operations are controlled by classical hardware, which generates and processes the signals required to manipulate qubits. Efficient interfaces between classical and quantum systems are essential for the seamless execution of quantum algorithms. This integration poses significant engineering challenges, given the need for precise timing and synchronization.

Scalability is the ultimate goal of quantum hardware and architecture development. Building quantum computers with thousands or millions of qubits is necessary to tackle problems beyond the capabilities of classical supercomputers. Achieving scalability requires advances in qubit fabrication, control, and error correction. Modular architectures, where smaller quantum processors are interconnected to form larger systems, offer a promising approach to scaling up quantum computers.

The choice of quantum hardware and architecture depends on the specific requirements of the intended application. For example, quantum simulators used in material science and chemistry may prioritize high coherence times and connectivity, while quantum communication networks may focus on the robustness of photonic qubits. Hybrid architectures that combine different types of qubits and technologies may also emerge, leveraging the strengths of each approach to create versatile and powerful quantum systems.

The rapid progress in quantum hardware and architectures is paving the way for practical quantum computing. Innovations in materials, fabrication techniques, and control systems are continually pushing the boundaries of what is possible. As researchers and engineers overcome the challenges of coherence, fidelity, connectivity, and error correction, the dream of building large-scale, fault-tolerant quantum computers moves closer to reality.

In conclusion, the development of quantum hardware and architectures is a dynamic and multifaceted field, driven by the quest to harness the power of quantum mechanics for computation. Each type of qubit technology offers unique advantages and faces distinct challenges, shaping the design and capabilities of quantum systems. The integration of classical and quantum systems, the implementation of error correction, and the pursuit of scalability are critical factors in the evolution of quantum architectures. As the field advances, the potential for quantum computers to revolutionize computation and solve previously intractable problems becomes increasingly tangible.

Quantum Algorithms and Programming

Quantum algorithms and programming represent the heart of quantum computing, offering the means to harness the extraordinary power of quantum mechanics for solving complex problems. Unlike classical algorithms, which rely on binary bits, quantum algorithms leverage qubits and the principles of superposition and entanglement to process information in fundamentally new ways. This chapter delves into the essential quantum algorithms, illustrating their unique capabilities and providing practical guidance for programming quantum computers.

A key advantage of quantum algorithms is their ability to perform certain computations exponentially faster than classical algorithms. Shor's algorithm for integer factorization and Grover's algorithm for unstructured search are prime examples of this quantum speedup. Shor's algorithm, developed by mathematician Peter Shor in 1994, can factor large integers exponentially faster than the best-known classical methods. This has profound implications for cryptography, as many encryption schemes rely on the difficulty of factorizing large numbers. Grover's algorithm, on the other hand, offers a quadratic speedup for searching unsorted databases, providing a significant advantage in fields like data mining and optimization.

To understand how these algorithms work, it's essential to grasp the basics of quantum gates and circuits. Quantum gates are the building blocks of quantum algorithms, analogous to classical logic gates. They manipulate qubits by altering their states through unitary operations. Common quantum gates include the Hadamard gate, which creates superposition states; the Pauli-X gate, which flips the state of a qubit; and the CNOT gate, which entangles pairs of qubits. By combining these gates in various sequences, complex quantum circuits can be constructed to perform specific computations.

Programming quantum computers requires a shift in mindset from classical programming. Quantum programming languages, such as Qiskit, Cirq, and Q#, provide the tools needed to design and execute quantum algorithms. These languages allow developers to define quantum circuits, simulate their behavior, and run them on actual quantum hardware. A typical quantum program involves initializing qubits, applying a series of quantum gates, and measuring the final states of the qubits to obtain the result.

One of the most exciting aspects of quantum programming is the opportunity to explore quantum entanglement and superposition. Entanglement is a phenomenon where qubits become interconnected, such that the state of one qubit instantly affects the state of another, regardless of the distance between them. This property is harnessed in many quantum algorithms to achieve parallelism and speedup. Superposition, on the other hand, allows qubits to exist in multiple states simultaneously, enabling the exploration of many possible solutions at once.

Implementing Shor's algorithm on a quantum computer involves several steps. First, the number to be factorized is encoded into the quantum register. Next, a quantum Fourier transform is applied, creating a superposition of states that represent the possible factors. Quantum gates are then used to interfere these states in a way that amplifies the probabilities of the correct factors. Finally, a measurement collapses the superposition, revealing the factors. While the full implementation requires a large number of qubits and high-fidelity gates, simplified versions of Shor's algorithm can be run on current quantum hardware to demonstrate its principles.

Grover's algorithm, in contrast, is more straightforward to implement on near-term quantum devices. The algorithm begins by preparing a superposition of all possible states in the search space. It then iteratively applies two main operations: the Grover diffusion operator and the oracle. The oracle marks the solution state by flipping its phase, while the diffusion operator amplifies the probability of the marked state. After a specific number of iterations, the algorithm concludes with a measurement that reveals the solution with high probability.

Beyond Shor's and Grover's algorithms, there are numerous other quantum algorithms with potential applications in various fields. Quantum simulation algorithms, for instance, can model the behavior of quantum systems, providing insights into chemistry, material science, and fundamental physics. Quantum machine learning algorithms aim to enhance classical machine learning techniques by leveraging quantum parallelism and entanglement. Optimization algorithms, such as the Quantum Approximate Optimization Algorithm (QAOA), seek to find optimal solutions to complex problems more efficiently than classical methods.

For beginners entering the field of quantum programming, it is essential to start with a solid foundation in linear algebra and quantum mechanics. Understanding concepts such as vector spaces, eigenvalues, and unitary transformations is crucial for grasping how quantum algorithms operate. Many online resources, including tutorials and courses, are available to help build this foundational knowledge.

Practicing with quantum programming languages is also vital. Platforms like IBM's Quantum Experience offer cloud-based access to quantum computers, allowing users to run their quantum programs on real hardware. Experimenting with simple quantum circuits and gradually tackling more complex algorithms can build confidence and proficiency in quantum programming.

Collaboration and community engagement play a significant role in advancing one's understanding of quantum computing. Participating in forums, attending workshops, and joining quantum computing groups can provide valuable insights and support. Collaborating with peers and experts helps in overcoming challenges and staying updated with the latest developments in the field.

As quantum hardware continues to evolve, the field of quantum algorithms and programming will undoubtedly expand, unlocking new possibilities and applications. The journey from understanding basic quantum principles to implementing sophisticated quantum algorithms is both challenging and rewarding. With perseverance and curiosity, beginners can contribute to the exciting frontier of quantum computing, paving the way for groundbreaking discoveries and innovations.

In conclusion, mastering quantum algorithms and programming requires a deep understanding of quantum mechanics, proficiency in quantum programming languages, and hands-on experience with quantum hardware. By exploring foundational algorithms like Shor's and Grover's, and engaging with the quantum computing community, beginners can develop the skills needed to navigate this rapidly advancing field. The potential of quantum computing to revolutionize various industries makes the pursuit of knowledge in this area a worthwhile and exciting endeavor.

Quantum Error Correction

Quantum error correction is an essential pillar in the development of practical quantum computers. Unlike classical computers, which rely on bits that are either 0 or 1, quantum computers use qubits that can exist in superpositions of states. This unique property enables powerful computations but also makes qubits extremely vulnerable to errors from environmental noise, imperfect gate operations, and other quantum decoherence sources. To achieve reliable quantum computation, it is crucial to devise methods that detect and correct errors without measuring the qubits directly, thereby preserving their quantum state.

The concept of quantum error correction is rooted in classical error correction theory but is significantly more complex due to the nature of quantum information. Classical error correction uses redundancy, encoding information across multiple bits, allowing errors to be detected and corrected by comparing redundant copies. Quantum error correction adapts this idea but faces the challenge of maintaining quantum coherence and dealing with both bit-flip and phase-flip errors.

One of the foundational techniques in quantum error correction is the use of quantum error-correcting codes. These codes encode a logical qubit into a set of physical qubits, creating redundancy that allows detection and correction of errors. The simplest example is the three-qubit bit-flip code, which protects against bit-flip errors. In this code, a logical qubit state . If one of the qubits undergoes a bit-flip error, majority voting can be used to identify and correct the error, restoring the original logical qubit state.

However, bit-flip errors are only one type of error that qubits can experience. Phase-flip errors, where the phase of the qubit state is altered, are equally problematic. The nine-qubit Shor code is an early and more comprehensive quantum error-correcting code that addresses both bit-flip and phase-flip errors. This code encodes a single logical qubit into nine physical qubits, using a combination of bit-flip and phase-flip error correction techniques to protect the logical qubit from both types of errors simultaneously.

A more practical and widely used approach in modern quantum error correction is the surface code. Surface codes are topological codes that arrange qubits on a two-dimensional lattice, where each qubit interacts only with its nearest neighbors. This local interaction structure simplifies the implementation and scaling of quantum error correction. Surface codes use a combination of plaquette operators to detect errors, allowing for efficient and robust error correction. The surface code is highly scalable and is considered one of the leading candidates for realizing fault-tolerant quantum computation.

The implementation of quantum error correction requires additional qubits for encoding logical qubits and performing error detection and correction operations. This overhead is a significant engineering challenge, as the number of physical qubits required can be an order of magnitude higher than the number of logical qubits. For instance, achieving fault tolerance with surface codes typically requires thousands of physical qubits to reliably encode a single logical qubit. Advances in qubit technology, error rates, and error correction algorithms are essential to reduce this overhead and make large-scale quantum computing feasible.

Quantum error correction also involves the use of syndrome measurements to detect errors without collapsing the quantum state. These measurements provide information about the presence and type of errors, allowing for appropriate corrective actions. A crucial aspect of syndrome measurements is that they must be designed to extract error information without revealing the encoded logical qubit's state, preserving the superposition and entanglement necessary for quantum computation.

One of the most significant theoretical achievements in quantum error correction is the threshold theorem. This theorem states that if the error rate per qubit and gate operation is below a certain threshold, it is possible to perform arbitrary long quantum computations reliably using quantum error correction. The exact value of this threshold depends on the specific error-correcting code and the error model but is typically on the order of 10^{-3} to 10^{-2}. Achieving and maintaining error rates below this threshold is a primary goal in the development of quantum hardware.

Practical implementation of quantum error correction also requires real-time error detection and correction. Classical control systems must process syndrome measurements, identify the errors, and apply corrective operations swiftly to prevent error accumulation. This integration of classical and quantum systems introduces additional complexity, demanding fast and reliable classical hardware and algorithms to support quantum error correction.

The future of quantum error correction lies in continuous improvement of error-correcting codes, qubit coherence times, and gate fidelities. Researchers are exploring new codes, such as low-density parity-check (LDPC) codes and color codes, which promise more efficient error correction with lower overhead. Advances in materials science and qubit design aim to enhance qubit coherence, reducing the frequency of errors. Improved gate fidelities, achieved through better control techniques and error mitigation strategies, further enhance the prospects of fault-tolerant quantum computation.

Understanding quantum error correction is essential for anyone entering the field of quantum computing. It provides the foundation for building reliable quantum systems capable of executing complex algorithms without succumbing to errors. As the field progresses, the principles and techniques of quantum error correction will continue to evolve, driven by both theoretical insights and practical advancements in quantum hardware.

In sum, quantum error correction is a cornerstone of quantum computing, addressing the inherent fragility of qubits and enabling the reliable execution of quantum algorithms. Through sophisticated encoding schemes, syndrome measurements, and real-time error correction, it transforms the promise of quantum computation into a practical reality. As research and technology advance, the challenges of implementing large-scale quantum error correction will be met, paving the way for robust and scalable quantum computers. The journey to fault-tolerant quantum computation is arduous but essential, and the progress made in this area will ultimately unlock the full potential of quantum technology.

Challenges in Quantum Hardware Development

Developing quantum hardware presents a myriad of challenges that must be overcome to realize the full potential of quantum computing. These challenges span a wide range of disciplines, including physics, engineering, and computer science. Each qubit technology, whether based on superconducting circuits, trapped ions, or other physical systems, brings its own set of obstacles. However, common themes such as qubit coherence, error rates, scalability, and control systems are critical to all approaches.

One of the primary challenges in quantum hardware development is maintaining qubit coherence. Qubits, the fundamental units of quantum information, are incredibly sensitive to their environment. They can easily lose their quantum state due to interactions with external fields, thermal fluctuations, and other qubits. This phenomenon, known as decoherence, limits the time during which quantum information can be reliably stored and manipulated. Various strategies are employed to enhance coherence times, such as operating qubits at extremely low temperatures to reduce thermal noise or using sophisticated shielding techniques to block external electromagnetic interference.

For superconducting qubits, which are among the most advanced qubit technologies, coherence times have steadily improved over the years. These qubits are typically operated at millikelvin temperatures using dilution refrigerators. However, even in these controlled environments, achieving long coherence times remains a significant challenge. Researchers continually seek materials with lower intrinsic noise and develop new qubit designs that are less susceptible to decoherence.

Trapped ion qubits, another leading technology, also face coherence challenges. These qubits are individual ions confined and manipulated using electromagnetic fields in ultra-high vacuum chambers. While trapped ions boast relatively long coherence times compared to other qubit types, they require extremely precise control of laser systems and electromagnetic fields. Any instability in these control systems can lead to decoherence and loss of quantum information.

Another major hurdle in quantum hardware development is error rates during qubit operations. Quantum gates, the fundamental operations that manipulate qubits, must be performed with high fidelity to ensure accurate computation. However, imperfections in control signals, cross-talk between qubits, and other noise sources contribute to errors. Minimizing these errors is crucial, as even small error rates can accumulate rapidly in quantum algorithms, leading to incorrect results.

To address this, researchers focus on improving the precision of control electronics and developing error mitigation techniques. For superconducting qubits, this involves refining microwave pulse sequences and optimizing the design of qubit circuits to minimize unwanted interactions. In the case of trapped ions, it requires enhancing the stability and accuracy of laser systems used for qubit manipulation.

Scalability is another formidable challenge in quantum hardware development. Building a quantum computer capable of solving practical problems requires scaling up from a few qubits to thousands or even millions of qubits. This scaling must be achieved while maintaining low error rates and long coherence times. The complexity of control systems and the physical layout of qubits become increasingly difficult to manage as the number of qubits grows.

One approach to scalability is the modular design of quantum processors. Instead of building a monolithic quantum computer, researchers are exploring architectures that connect smaller quantum modules. Each module contains a manageable number of qubits that can be controlled and measured independently.

The modules are then linked together using quantum communication techniques, such as quantum teleportation or entanglement swapping, to perform larger-scale computations.

In addition to modular designs, researchers are investigating new materials and fabrication techniques to improve qubit performance and scalability. For superconducting qubits, this includes exploring different superconducting materials, such as niobium or aluminum, and developing advanced lithography techniques to create smaller and more precise qubit circuits. For trapped ions, it involves designing more efficient ion traps and integrating photonic components for scalable quantum communication.

The development of robust quantum control systems is also crucial for scaling up quantum hardware. These systems must precisely generate and deliver control signals to qubits, perform error correction, and manage data flow between classical and quantum processors. As the number of qubits increases, the complexity of control systems grows exponentially, requiring significant advancements in both hardware and software.

Cryogenic control systems are essential for superconducting qubits, as they operate at temperatures near absolute zero. These systems must maintain stable temperatures and provide reliable cooling for qubits and their control electronics. Innovations in cryogenic engineering, such as more efficient dilution refrigerators and cryocoolers, are vital to support large-scale quantum processors.

For trapped ion qubits, the challenge lies in developing scalable laser systems and vacuum technologies. High-power, stable lasers are required to manipulate ions, and maintaining ultra-high vacuum conditions becomes more difficult as the size of the ion trap array increases. Advances in laser technology, such as the development of compact, tunable lasers, and improvements in vacuum chamber design, are critical to overcoming these challenges.

Another aspect of quantum hardware development is the integration of quantum and classical systems. Quantum computers rely on classical processors to perform error correction, control qubit operations, and interpret measurement results. Efficiently interfacing quantum processors with classical hardware is essential for practical quantum computation. This involves developing high-speed, low-latency communication links and designing control systems that can handle the massive data flow between quantum and classical components.

Moreover, the field of quantum hardware development faces significant engineering challenges related to fabrication and assembly. Creating high-quality qubits and quantum circuits requires advanced nanofabrication techniques with precise control over material properties and dimensions. Any defects or impurities in the materials can introduce errors and degrade qubit performance. Therefore, researchers continuously strive to improve fabrication processes and develop new techniques for assembling quantum hardware with atomic-scale precision.

The journey towards practical quantum computers also involves addressing the challenge of qubit connectivity. In many quantum algorithms, qubits need to interact with each other to perform entanglement and gate operations. Ensuring robust and low-latency connectivity between qubits is essential for efficient quantum computation. This requires designing qubit layouts and interconnects that minimize cross-talk and maximize the fidelity of quantum operations.

Despite the numerous challenges, the progress in quantum hardware development is remarkable. Researchers worldwide are making significant strides in improving qubit coherence, reducing error rates, and developing scalable architectures. Collaborative efforts between physicists, engineers, and computer scientists are driving innovations that bring us closer to realizing practical quantum computers.

In summary, developing quantum hardware is a complex and multifaceted endeavor that involves overcoming challenges related to qubit coherence, error rates, scalability, and control systems. Each qubit technology presents unique obstacles, but common themes such as enhancing coherence times, minimizing errors, and developing scalable architectures are central to all approaches. As research and technology advance, the barriers to practical quantum computation will continue to diminish, paving the way for the next generation of computing. The journey is challenging, but the potential rewards of unlocking the power of quantum computing make it a pursuit worth every effort.

Chapter 3: Quantum Computing Technologies

Superconducting Quantum Computers

Superconducting quantum computers are at the forefront of quantum computing research, offering a promising path toward practical quantum computing. These systems leverage the principles of superconductivity to create and manipulate qubits, the fundamental units of quantum information. Superconducting qubits are typically fabricated using circuits made of superconducting materials, such as aluminum or niobium, which exhibit zero electrical resistance at cryogenic temperatures.

One of the key features of superconducting qubits is their ability to maintain quantum coherence for relatively long periods, though still far shorter than what's achievable with classical bits. Quantum coherence is essential for performing quantum operations and maintaining the superposition states that give quantum computers their power. However, maintaining coherence is challenging because qubits are highly sensitive to their environment, which can cause decoherence and errors.

The most common type of superconducting qubit is the transmon, which is a refined version of the earlier Cooper-pair box qubit. Transmons are designed to be less sensitive to charge noise, which was a significant problem in earlier designs. They achieve this by increasing the ratio of the Josephson energy to the charging energy, thereby reducing sensitivity to fluctuations in the charge environment. This design improvement has made transmons one of the most widely used qubit types in current quantum computing research.

Superconducting qubits are typically operated at temperatures close to absolute zero, around 10 millikelvin, using dilution refrigerators. These extremely low temperatures are necessary to achieve superconductivity and minimize thermal noise, which can disrupt qubit operations. The cooling systems required for superconducting quantum computers are complex and expensive, representing a significant engineering challenge. Nonetheless, advances in cryogenic technology continue to improve the efficiency and reliability of these systems.

Creating and controlling superconducting qubits involves sophisticated nanofabrication techniques. The qubits are patterned on silicon or sapphire substrates using electron-beam lithography and other advanced techniques. The precision required in the fabrication process is immense, as even minor imperfections can significantly impact qubit performance. Researchers continuously refine these techniques to enhance qubit quality and yield.

Once fabricated, superconducting qubits need to be precisely controlled to perform quantum operations. Control systems use microwave pulses to manipulate qubit states and perform quantum gates. The design and calibration of these microwave pulses are critical for achieving high-fidelity operations. Errors in pulse shaping or timing can lead to gate errors, which accumulate over the course of a quantum algorithm and degrade the final result.

To mitigate errors, researchers employ various error correction and mitigation techniques. Quantum error correction involves encoding quantum information into a larger number of physical qubits, creating redundancy that allows for the detection and correction of errors. Implementing error correction is a formidable challenge, requiring the development of efficient error-correcting codes and the ability to perform error correction operations without introducing additional errors.

Another promising approach to reducing errors is the development of error mitigation techniques, which do not require full error correction but instead aim to reduce the impact of errors on quantum computations. These techniques include error extrapolation, where the results of quantum computations at different error rates are used to estimate the zero-error result, and randomized compiling, which averages out coherent errors by randomizing the sequence of quantum gates.

Scalability is a major concern in the development of superconducting quantum computers. Current systems contain tens to hundreds of qubits, but practical quantum computing will require thousands or millions of qubits. Scaling up involves addressing several challenges, including qubit connectivity, control system complexity, and error rates. One approach to scaling is the use of modular architectures, where smaller quantum processors are connected to form a larger system. This modular approach can help manage the complexity of control systems and improve fault tolerance.

Qubit connectivity is crucial for performing multi-qubit operations and implementing quantum error correction. In superconducting quantum computers, qubits are typically arranged in a 2D grid, with nearest-neighbor interactions facilitated by microwave resonators or direct coupling. Researchers are exploring 3D integration and other advanced interconnect technologies to improve connectivity and reduce cross-talk between qubits.

The control systems for superconducting quantum computers must be both precise and scalable. These systems include microwave generators, digital-to-analog converters, and feedback mechanisms for real-time error correction. Integrating these components into a scalable architecture requires careful design to minimize latency and noise. Advances in classical control electronics, such as the development of application-specific integrated circuits (ASICs) for quantum control, are essential for achieving the necessary performance and scalability.

Another important aspect of superconducting quantum computers is their readout systems, which measure the state of qubits at the end of a computation. Readout is typically performed using dispersive measurement techniques, where the state of a qubit shifts the frequency of a coupled resonator, allowing for state detection via microwave signals. High-fidelity readout is critical for accurate quantum computation, and researchers are continually improving readout techniques to achieve better performance.

Despite the challenges, superconducting quantum computers have demonstrated significant progress. In recent years, researchers have achieved increasingly complex quantum algorithms and demonstrated the potential for quantum advantage in certain tasks. Quantum advantage refers to the ability of a quantum computer to solve a problem faster than the best classical algorithms. Achieving and demonstrating quantum advantage is a major milestone in the field and drives ongoing research and development.

Collaborations between academia, industry, and government are crucial for advancing superconducting quantum computing. These collaborations bring together expertise from various fields and provide the resources needed to tackle the multifaceted challenges of quantum hardware development. Large-scale projects and consortia, such as the Quantum Economic Development Consortium (QED-C) and the European Quantum Flagship, play a pivotal role in fostering innovation and accelerating progress.

In conclusion, superconducting quantum computers represent a leading approach to realizing practical quantum computing. They leverage the unique properties of superconducting materials to create and manipulate qubits with high precision. The development of these systems involves overcoming significant challenges related to qubit coherence, error rates, scalability, and control systems. Advances in nanofabrication, cryogenics, microwave engineering, and error correction are driving the field forward. While many obstacles remain, the progress to date is promising, and the potential benefits of quantum computing make it a pursuit of great scientific and technological importance. The journey toward practical superconducting quantum computers is complex and demanding, but the potential to revolutionize computing and solve problems beyond the reach of classical systems makes it a highly worthwhile endeavor.

Trapped Ion Quantum Computers

Trapped ion quantum computers represent one of the most promising and well-researched approaches to quantum computing. This technology leverages individual ions, which are atomic particles with an electric charge, to serve as qubits. These ions are confined and manipulated using electromagnetic fields within a vacuum chamber. The precision and stability offered by trapped ion systems make them an attractive candidate for scalable quantum computing.

The journey begins with the trapping of ions. Typically, ions are created by ionizing atoms from elements like ytterbium or calcium. Once ionized, these atoms are held in place using a combination of static electric fields, which form what is known as a Paul trap or a Penning trap. In a Paul trap, oscillating electric fields create a dynamic potential well that confines the ions, while in a Penning trap, static magnetic and electric fields are used for confinement. The ions, once trapped, can be cooled to near absolute zero using laser cooling techniques, which significantly reduce their thermal motion and allow for precise control over their quantum states.

Each ion in the trap represents a qubit, with its quantum state defined by the energy levels of its electrons. The two levels typically used are the ground state and an excited state, or two hyperfine states of the ion. Transitions between these states can be induced using laser pulses, which serve as the primary means of manipulating the qubits. The precise control afforded by laser systems allows for the implementation of single-qubit gates, which are the building blocks of quantum algorithms.

To implement quantum computations, it's essential to perform not only single-qubit operations but also multi-qubit gates. In trapped ion systems, this is often achieved through the use of the collective motion of the ions. By applying specific laser pulses, researchers can entangle the states of two or more ions, creating a controlled-NOT (CNOT) gate or other entangling operations. This process leverages the shared motional states of the ions, effectively using the trap's vibrational modes as a bus to mediate interactions between qubits.

One of the significant advantages of trapped ion systems is their long coherence times. The quantum states of ions can remain stable for extended periods, often reaching seconds or longer. This stability is crucial for performing complex quantum algorithms, as it allows for a greater number of operations before decoherence and errors accumulate. However, maintaining coherence requires careful isolation from environmental noise and precise control over experimental conditions.

Error correction is another critical component of trapped ion quantum computing. Even with long coherence times, errors due to decoherence, imperfect gate operations, and other factors can still occur. Quantum error correction codes, such as the surface code or the Bacon-Shor code, are employed to detect and correct these errors. Implementing these codes in trapped ion systems involves encoding logical qubits across multiple physical qubits and performing frequent error-checking operations without disturbing the encoded information.

Scalability is a central challenge for all quantum computing platforms, and trapped ion systems are no exception. Current systems, which typically contain tens of ions, need to be scaled up to thousands or millions of qubits to solve practical problems beyond the reach of classical computers. Various strategies are being explored to achieve this scaling. One approach is the use of segmented traps, where ions can be shuttled between different regions of the trap for processing and storage. Another approach involves the use of photonic interconnects, where entanglement is generated between ions in separate traps using photons, effectively linking multiple smaller quantum processors into a larger network.

The control systems required for trapped ion quantum computing are sophisticated and demand high precision. Laser systems must be precisely tuned and stabilized to ensure accurate qubit manipulation. Additionally, the electronic control systems that generate the trapping fields and detect the ion states must operate with minimal noise and high fidelity. Advances in laser technology, electronics, and feedback control systems are continually improving the performance and reliability of trapped ion quantum computers.

One of the most compelling aspects of trapped ion quantum computing is its potential for high-fidelity quantum operations. Experimental demonstrations have achieved single-qubit gate fidelities exceeding 99.9% and two-qubit gate fidelities over 99%. These high fidelities are essential for practical quantum computing, as they reduce the overhead required for error correction and allow for more complex computations to be performed before errors become problematic.

Despite the challenges, the progress in trapped ion quantum computing has been remarkable. Recent experiments have demonstrated the ability to perform quantum algorithms with dozens of qubits, including small-scale implementations of quantum error correction and simulations of quantum systems. These achievements highlight the potential of trapped ion systems to advance the field of quantum computing and bring us closer to realizing practical quantum computers.

Collaboration between academic institutions, industry, and government agencies is driving rapid advancements in this field. Large-scale research initiatives and consortia are fostering innovation and providing the resources needed to tackle the complex challenges of building scalable trapped ion quantum computers. These collaborations are crucial for integrating the diverse expertise required, from quantum physics and engineering to computer science and materials science.

The future of trapped ion quantum computing is both exciting and demanding. The path to practical quantum computers involves overcoming significant technical hurdles, but the potential rewards are immense. Quantum computers have the potential to revolutionize fields ranging from cryptography and materials science to drug discovery and artificial intelligence. The work being done today in trapped ion systems is laying the foundation for this future, pushing the boundaries of what is possible and opening new avenues for exploration and discovery.

In conclusion, trapped ion quantum computers offer a promising route to realizing the immense potential of quantum computing. They combine long coherence times, high-fidelity operations, and the ability to precisely control and entangle qubits. The journey involves sophisticated experimental techniques, cutting-edge technology, and innovative approaches to scalability and error correction. As researchers continue to make strides in this field, the dream of practical quantum computing comes ever closer to reality, promising to transform our understanding of computation and solve problems that were once thought intractable.

Topological Quantum Computers

Topological quantum computers represent a fascinating and potentially revolutionary approach to quantum computing, leveraging the exotic properties of quasiparticles known as anyons to achieve robust quantum computation. Unlike other quantum computing platforms that rely on the fragile quantum states of individual particles, topological quantum computers use the global properties of these particles' braiding patterns in space-time to store and process information. This unique approach offers inherent protection against local errors, promising a more stable and scalable path to realizing practical quantum computers.

The concept of topological quantum computing is deeply rooted in the principles of topology, a branch of mathematics concerned with the properties of space that are preserved under continuous deformations. In simple terms, topology studies the global properties of objects that remain unchanged even when the objects are stretched, twisted, or deformed. This mathematical framework is crucial for understanding how topological quantum computers work.

At the heart of topological quantum computing are anyons, particularly non-Abelian anyons, which exhibit unusual statistical behaviors that differ from those of standard fermions and bosons. These anyons can only exist in two-dimensional systems, such as those found in certain fractional quantum Hall states or in the surface states of topological superconductors. When anyons are exchanged or braided around each other, their quantum states undergo transformations that are dependent on the entire history of their braiding paths, rather than just their final positions. This history-dependent property is key to encoding and manipulating quantum information in a topologically protected manner.

To create a topological quantum computer, one must first realize a physical system that supports non-Abelian anyons. One promising candidate is the topological superconductor, which can host Majorana zero modes at its edges or at the cores of vortices. These Majorana modes are particularly attractive because they are predicted to exhibit non-Abelian statistics, making them suitable for topological quantum computation. Experimental efforts are focused on engineering such systems using materials like spin-orbit coupled semiconductors in proximity to conventional superconductors, or by exploring intrinsic topological superconductors.

Once a suitable system is realized, the next step is to manipulate the anyons to perform quantum computations. In topological quantum computing, qubits are encoded in the collective states of pairs of anyons. Quantum gates are implemented by braiding these anyons around each other in specific patterns. The topological nature of these braidings ensures that the resulting quantum operations are robust against local perturbations, such as thermal noise or slight imperfections in the system. This robustness is a significant advantage over other quantum computing approaches, where maintaining coherence and correcting errors can be challenging.

The braiding operations required for topological quantum gates are inherently non-local, meaning they involve the global properties of the system rather than local interactions. This non-locality is what provides the topological protection against errors, as local disturbances cannot easily affect the global braiding patterns. However, implementing these braiding operations in practice requires precise control over the system and the ability to move anyons around without introducing unwanted errors. Researchers are developing various techniques to achieve this control, including using external magnetic fields, electrical gates, or even mechanical manipulation.

One of the most intriguing aspects of topological quantum computing is its potential for fault-tolerant quantum computation. Fault tolerance is a critical requirement for practical quantum computers, as it ensures that computations can proceed accurately even in the presence of errors. The topological nature of anyon braiding provides a built-in form of error protection, reducing the need for extensive error correction codes. However, additional error correction methods may still be necessary to deal with higher-level errors or imperfections in the system. These methods typically involve encoding logical qubits into more complex topological states and using a combination of braiding and measurement-based techniques to detect and correct errors.

Despite its promise, topological quantum computing is still in its early stages, with many challenges to overcome before it can be realized on a large scale. One major challenge is the experimental verification and manipulation of non-Abelian anyons, which requires sophisticated techniques and precise control over the physical systems. Another challenge is scaling up the system to support a large number of qubits and complex quantum operations. Researchers are exploring various approaches to address these challenges, including hybrid systems that combine topological qubits with other types of qubits, as well as new materials and fabrication techniques to create more robust and scalable topological systems.

The potential impact of topological quantum computing extends beyond the realm of quantum computation itself. The study of topological phases of matter and anyons has led to new insights into fundamental physics, with potential applications in areas such as quantum field theory, condensed matter physics, and even cosmology. The interdisciplinary nature of this research is driving collaborations between physicists, material scientists, mathematicians, and engineers, fostering a vibrant and dynamic field of study.

As we continue to explore the possibilities of topological quantum computing, it is essential to keep in mind the broader context of quantum technology development. While topological quantum computers offer unique advantages, they are just one part of the larger quantum ecosystem. Advances in other quantum computing platforms, such as superconducting qubits, trapped ions, and photonic systems, are also crucial for building a diverse and robust quantum technology landscape. Each approach has its own strengths and challenges, and the interplay between different technologies will likely play a significant role in the future of quantum computing.

In conclusion, topological quantum computers represent a novel and promising approach to achieving practical quantum computation. By leveraging the unique properties of non-Abelian anyons and topological phases of matter, these systems offer inherent protection against local errors and the potential for fault-tolerant quantum computation. The path to realizing topological quantum computers involves overcoming significant experimental and theoretical challenges, but the potential rewards are immense. As research progresses, the insights gained from studying topological quantum systems will continue to enrich our understanding of quantum physics and drive innovation in quantum technology.

Photonic Quantum Computers

Photonic quantum computers harness the unique properties of light to perform quantum computations. Unlike traditional computers that use electrical signals to encode information, photonic quantum computers use photons, the elementary particles of light, as their qubits. Photons are particularly appealing for quantum computing because they are resistant to decoherence, can travel long distances without losing information, and can be easily manipulated using linear optical elements. These characteristics make photonic quantum computing a promising candidate for scalable and practical quantum computation.

The fundamental building block of a photonic quantum computer is the photonic qubit. A photonic qubit can be represented in various ways, such as the polarization state of a photon (horizontal or vertical), the path a photon takes, or even the time of arrival of the photon. These different representations allow for versatile means of encoding and manipulating quantum information. Polarization, for instance, is a straightforward method where a horizontally polarized photon represents the logical state $|0\rangle$, and a vertically polarized photon represents the logical state $|1\rangle$.

Generating and controlling photons with high precision is essential for photonic quantum computing. This is typically achieved using laser sources, which can produce single photons or entangled pairs of photons through processes like spontaneous parametric down-conversion (SPDC) or four-wave mixing. Once generated, these photons need to be manipulated to perform quantum logic operations. Linear optical elements such as beamsplitters, waveplates, and phase shifters are used to control the path and polarization of photons, implementing single-qubit gates and creating superpositions.

Entanglement is a crucial resource for quantum computation, and photonic systems excel at creating and manipulating entangled states. Entangled photons can be generated using SPDC, where a single photon splits into a pair of entangled photons. These entangled pairs can be used to implement two-qubit gates, which are necessary for universal quantum computation. One common two-qubit gate in photonic systems is the controlled-NOT (CNOT) gate, which can be realized using a combination of beamsplitters, phase shifters, and single-photon detectors.

Measurement plays a pivotal role in photonic quantum computing. Unlike other quantum systems where qubits can be directly manipulated and read out, photonic qubits often require measurement-based techniques to perform computations. This approach involves entangling photons, performing measurements on a subset of them, and using the outcomes to influence subsequent operations. This measurement-based model, also known as cluster-state or one-way quantum computing, offers a different paradigm compared to traditional circuit-based quantum computing.

A significant advantage of photonic quantum computers is their potential for integration with existing fiber-optic communication infrastructure. Photons can travel through optical fibers with minimal loss, making it feasible to create large-scale quantum networks. These networks could link multiple photonic quantum processors, enabling distributed quantum computing and quantum communication over long distances. Quantum key distribution (QKD) is an example of a practical application where photonic systems already provide secure communication channels using the principles of quantum mechanics.

Despite these advantages, photonic quantum computing faces several challenges. One of the primary obstacles is the probabilistic nature of photon interactions. Many linear optical operations used to implement quantum gates rely on probabilistic processes, which means that successful gate operations may occur only a fraction of the time. This probabilistic behavior can be mitigated using techniques like post-selection, where only successful events are kept, but this approach reduces the overall efficiency of the computation.

Another challenge is the integration of photonic components into scalable architectures. While individual photonic elements like beamsplitters and waveplates are well understood, creating large-scale, integrated photonic circuits requires precise fabrication techniques and robust error correction methods. Researchers are exploring various platforms for photonic integration, including silicon photonics, which leverages the mature silicon fabrication technology used in classical computer chips, and other materials like indium phosphide and lithium niobate.

Error correction in photonic quantum computing is an active area of research. The inherent resilience of photons to decoherence is advantageous, but other sources of error, such as photon loss and imperfect gate operations, still need to be addressed. Quantum error correction codes, such as the surface code or the bosonic code, are being adapted for photonic systems. These codes encode logical qubits into entangled states of multiple physical qubits, allowing for the detection and correction of errors without destroying the quantum information.

Recent advancements in photonic quantum computing have demonstrated the feasibility of small-scale quantum algorithms and protocols. For instance, researchers have successfully implemented Shor's algorithm and Grover's search algorithm using photonic systems, showcasing the potential of this approach for solving computational problems. Additionally, photonic quantum simulators have been used to model complex quantum systems, providing insights into phenomena that are difficult to study using classical computers.

The development of photonic quantum computers is driven by interdisciplinary collaborations between physicists, engineers, and computer scientists. Innovations in photon source technology, photonic integration, and quantum algorithms are all contributing to the progress of the field. Startups and established companies are also entering the arena, bringing additional resources and expertise to the development of practical photonic quantum computing solutions.

Looking ahead, the roadmap for photonic quantum computing involves several key milestones. One critical goal is the demonstration of fault-tolerant quantum computation using photonic systems. Achieving this will require advances in error correction, efficient photon sources, and scalable integration techniques. Another important objective is the development of quantum networks that can link multiple photonic processors, enabling distributed quantum computation and secure communication.

The potential applications of photonic quantum computers are vast and varied. In addition to solving complex computational problems, photonic systems could revolutionize fields such as cryptography, optimization, and materials science. For example, quantum algorithms running on photonic hardware could optimize supply chains, model new drugs and materials at the quantum level, and provide unbreakable encryption for secure communication.

In summary, photonic quantum computers offer a unique and promising approach to quantum computation, leveraging the properties of light to encode, manipulate, and transmit quantum information. While challenges remain in scaling up these systems and overcoming probabilistic gate operations, the inherent advantages of photonic qubits, such as resistance to decoherence and compatibility with existing communication infrastructure, make them a compelling candidate for future quantum technologies. As research and development continue, the progress in photonic quantum computing will likely lead to new breakthroughs and applications, bringing us closer to the realization of practical and scalable quantum computers.

Hybrid Approaches and Future Directions

Hybrid approaches in quantum computing represent a powerful strategy for overcoming the limitations of individual quantum systems by combining different types of qubits and technologies. This integration can harness the unique advantages of various quantum platforms, leading to more robust, scalable, and versatile quantum computers. As we explore hybrid approaches, it's essential to understand the strengths and weaknesses of different quantum systems and how their combination can pave the way for future advancements in quantum technology.

One prominent hybrid approach involves combining superconducting qubits with photonic qubits. Superconducting qubits, which are circuits cooled to near absolute zero to exhibit quantum mechanical properties, are known for their fast gate operations and strong coupling to microwave photons. However, they are prone to decoherence and have relatively short coherence times. On the other hand, photonic qubits, which use light particles to store and transmit quantum information, have long coherence times and can travel long distances with minimal loss, making them ideal for communication. By integrating these two platforms, researchers can create systems where superconducting qubits perform rapid computations while photonic qubits handle long-distance communication and entanglement distribution.

The interface between superconducting qubits and photonic qubits typically involves microwave-to-optical transducers. These devices convert quantum information from microwave photons, used by superconducting qubits, to optical photons, used by photonic qubits. Achieving efficient and low-noise conversion is challenging but crucial for creating a seamless hybrid system. Advances in materials science and nanofabrication are driving progress in this area, with researchers developing various approaches such as electro-optic modulators and optomechanical devices.

Another compelling hybrid approach integrates trapped ions with superconducting qubits. Trapped ions, which use electromagnetic fields to confine ions in a vacuum, are renowned for their long coherence times and high-fidelity operations. They excel in applications requiring precision and stability. However, scaling up trapped ion systems to large numbers of qubits is challenging due to the complexity of controlling many ions simultaneously. Superconducting qubits, with their ease of fabrication and scalability, can complement trapped ions by providing a platform for rapid, high-density quantum processing. Linking these two systems can be achieved through shared quantum memories or direct coupling mechanisms, potentially enabling large-scale quantum computations with high precision.

Hybrid quantum systems also explore the combination of different types of matter qubits. For instance, integrating spin qubits in semiconductors with superconducting qubits can leverage the long coherence times of spin qubits and the fast gate operations of superconducting qubits. Spin qubits, which use the magnetic spin of electrons or nuclei to represent quantum information, can be manipulated using magnetic fields and microwave pulses. Hybrid systems can use superconducting qubits for rapid quantum operations and spin qubits for long-term storage, creating a powerful combination for quantum computing and memory applications.

One of the key challenges in hybrid quantum computing is the development of efficient interconnects between different types of qubits. These interconnects must preserve quantum coherence and enable high-fidelity operations. Researchers are exploring various techniques, including quantum transduction, where quantum information is transferred between different physical systems, and hybrid quantum circuits, where different qubits are integrated on a single chip. Advancements in quantum control and error correction are also critical for ensuring the reliable operation of hybrid systems.

The future of hybrid quantum computing lies in the development of quantum networks, where different types of quantum processors are interconnected to form a distributed quantum computer. These networks can leverage the strengths of each platform, enabling complex quantum computations that are beyond the reach of individual systems. Quantum repeaters, which use entanglement swapping and purification techniques to extend the range of quantum communication, will play a crucial role in building scalable quantum networks. Hybrid approaches can integrate various types of qubits into these networks, enhancing their functionality and efficiency.

As hybrid quantum systems evolve, they will likely lead to new architectures and paradigms for quantum computing. For example, the concept of modular quantum computing envisions a network of smaller quantum processors, each optimized for specific tasks, working together to solve complex problems. This modular approach can overcome the limitations of monolithic quantum computers, offering greater flexibility and scalability. Researchers are also exploring hybrid quantum algorithms that combine different types of qubits and operations to achieve optimal performance for specific applications.

In addition to technical advancements, the success of hybrid quantum computing will depend on interdisciplinary collaboration among physicists, engineers, computer scientists, and material scientists. The integration of different quantum platforms requires a deep understanding of their underlying physics, as well as expertise in fabrication, control, and error correction. Collaboration across disciplines will drive innovation and accelerate the development of practical hybrid quantum systems.

Educational and training programs will also play a vital role in preparing the next generation of researchers and engineers for the challenges of hybrid quantum computing. As the field continues to evolve, there will be a growing need for professionals with expertise in multiple quantum platforms and the ability to integrate them into cohesive systems. Universities and research institutions are already expanding their quantum curriculum to include courses and hands-on training in hybrid quantum technologies.

The commercialization of hybrid quantum systems is another important aspect of future directions in quantum computing. Startups and established companies are investing in the development of hybrid quantum technologies, aiming to bring practical quantum solutions to the market. These efforts are supported by government funding and public-private partnerships, which recognize the strategic importance of quantum technology for national security, economic growth, and scientific advancement.

As we look to the future, hybrid quantum computing holds the promise of unlocking new frontiers in science and technology. From solving complex optimization problems and simulating quantum materials to enhancing cryptographic protocols and developing new pharmaceuticals, the potential applications of hybrid quantum systems are vast and varied. By combining the strengths of different quantum platforms, hybrid approaches can overcome current limitations and pave the way for practical, scalable, and versatile quantum computers.

In summary, hybrid approaches in quantum computing offer a powerful strategy for leveraging the unique advantages of different quantum platforms. By integrating superconducting qubits, photonic qubits, trapped ions, and other qubit types, researchers can create systems that are more robust, scalable, and versatile than any individual platform. The development of efficient interconnects, quantum networks, and modular architectures will drive the future of hybrid quantum computing, enabling new applications and scientific discoveries. Interdisciplinary collaboration, education, and commercialization efforts will be crucial for realizing the full potential of hybrid quantum systems, ushering in a new era of quantum technology.

Chapter 4: Quantum Algorithms and Applications

Quantum Simulation and Optimization

Quantum simulation and optimization represent two groundbreaking applications of quantum computing, offering the potential to solve complex problems that are intractable for classical computers. These fields harness the unique properties of quantum mechanics, such as superposition, entanglement, and quantum tunneling, to model and optimize systems beyond the reach of traditional methods.

Quantum simulation is particularly powerful in the realm of chemistry and materials science. Classical simulations of molecular structures and interactions are limited by the exponential growth of computational resources required as the system size increases. Quantum simulators, however, can naturally represent and manipulate these quantum states, providing a more direct and efficient approach. For instance, simulating the behavior of molecules like the nitrogenase enzyme, which is crucial for nitrogen fixation in plants, remains a formidable challenge for classical computers. Quantum simulators, leveraging qubits to represent electron states and their interactions, can potentially reveal insights into such complex biochemical processes, leading to advancements in agriculture and medicine.

The principles behind quantum simulation are elegantly simple yet profoundly different from classical approaches. At its core, a quantum simulator encodes the state of a quantum system into the state of a quantum computer. This encoding allows for the direct manipulation of quantum states, enabling the simulation of quantum dynamics in a way that classical bits cannot achieve. Quantum gates, analogous to classical logical gates, are used to evolve these states according to the rules of quantum mechanics.

Consider the example of simulating a simple molecule like hydrogen. In a quantum simulator, each electron state is represented by a qubit. The interactions between these qubits, governed by the Hamiltonian of the system, can be manipulated to mimic the behavior of the actual electrons in the molecule. By applying a sequence of quantum gates, we can simulate the evolution of the molecule over time, providing insights into its properties such as energy levels, bond lengths, and reaction pathways.

Quantum optimization, on the other hand, focuses on finding the best solution from a set of possible solutions, a task that is ubiquitous across various industries. From supply chain management and financial portfolio optimization to traffic flow and energy distribution, optimization problems are everywhere. Classical algorithms often struggle with these problems, especially when the solution space is vast and complex. Quantum optimization algorithms, such as the Quantum Approximate Optimization Algorithm (QAOA) and Variational Quantum Eigensolver (VQE), offer a promising alternative.

The QAOA, for instance, is designed to solve combinatorial optimization problems by leveraging quantum superposition and entanglement. It works by encoding the problem into a quantum state and using a parameterized quantum circuit to evolve this state towards the optimal solution. The parameters are adjusted iteratively based on classical feedback, gradually improving the solution quality. This hybrid approach, combining quantum and classical computation, allows QAOA to tackle problems like the Max-Cut problem or the Traveling Salesman Problem more efficiently than classical algorithms alone.

VQE, another powerful quantum optimization algorithm, is particularly suited for finding the ground state energy of a quantum system, a task crucial for quantum chemistry and materials science. It employs a variational approach, where a quantum computer prepares a trial wavefunction, and a classical optimizer adjusts the parameters to minimize the energy. The iterative process continues until the system converges to the ground state, providing valuable information about the system's properties.

To illustrate the practical impact of quantum optimization, consider the example of optimizing a financial portfolio. The goal is to maximize returns while minimizing risk, a problem that becomes exponentially complex as the number of assets increases. Traditional methods, based on mean-variance optimization, often struggle with large datasets and the need for accurate risk modeling. Quantum optimization algorithms can encode the portfolio optimization problem into a quantum state, exploring multiple configurations simultaneously and finding the optimal balance between risk and return more efficiently.

Beyond finance, quantum optimization has significant implications for logistics and supply chain management. For example, optimizing the routing of delivery trucks to minimize fuel consumption and delivery time involves solving a complex combinatorial problem. Quantum optimization algorithms can explore numerous routing possibilities simultaneously, identifying the most efficient routes and significantly reducing operational costs.

The potential of quantum simulation and optimization extends to fundamental science as well. In physics, quantum simulators can model exotic states of matter, such as topological insulators and high-temperature superconductors, aiding in the discovery of new materials with revolutionary properties. In biology, simulating protein folding processes can lead to breakthroughs in understanding diseases and developing new drugs. The ability to simulate and optimize complex systems at the quantum level opens up new frontiers in scientific research and technological innovation.

However, the practical implementation of quantum simulation and optimization is not without challenges. Current quantum hardware, while rapidly advancing, is still in the early stages of development. Issues such as qubit coherence times, gate fidelities, and error rates need to be addressed to realize the full potential of these algorithms. Nonetheless, ongoing research and development in quantum technologies are steadily overcoming these hurdles, bringing us closer to practical and scalable quantum computing solutions.

In preparation for the widespread adoption of quantum simulation and optimization, it is crucial for researchers, engineers, and industry professionals to develop a solid understanding of quantum principles and algorithms. Interdisciplinary collaboration between quantum physicists, computer scientists, and domain experts will be key to translating theoretical advancements into practical applications. Educational initiatives and training programs aimed at building quantum literacy will play a vital role in preparing the workforce for the quantum revolution.

In summary, quantum simulation and optimization represent transformative applications of quantum computing, offering unprecedented capabilities for modeling and solving complex problems across various domains. By harnessing the unique properties of quantum mechanics, these algorithms provide a significant advantage over classical methods, paving the way for breakthroughs in science, industry, and technology. As quantum hardware continues to evolve, the practical realization of these algorithms will unlock new possibilities, driving innovation and progress in ways we are only beginning to imagine.

Quantum Machine Learning

Quantum machine learning (QML) is an emerging field at the intersection of quantum computing and artificial intelligence. By leveraging the principles of quantum mechanics, QML aims to enhance traditional machine learning algorithms, offering potential speedups and improved performance for certain types of problems. This chapter delves into the foundational concepts of QML, explores its potential applications, and provides practical advice for those looking to venture into this exciting domain.

At its core, quantum machine learning seeks to utilize the unique properties of quantum computers—namely superposition, entanglement, and quantum interference—to process and analyze data in ways that classical computers cannot. Traditional machine learning algorithms, despite their success, often struggle with high-dimensional data and computationally intensive tasks. Quantum computers, with their ability to represent and manipulate large amounts of information simultaneously, offer a promising alternative.

One of the key concepts in QML is the quantum data encoding process. Classical data must be transformed into a quantum state, a process known as quantum feature mapping. This involves encoding classical bits into qubits, the fundamental units of quantum information. A common technique for this is amplitude encoding, where the amplitudes of a quantum state represent the data points. Another method is angle encoding, which uses the angles of qubit rotations to encode information. The choice of encoding method can significantly affect the performance of the quantum machine learning model.

Once the data is encoded into a quantum state, quantum algorithms can be applied to perform machine learning tasks. Quantum versions of classical algorithms, such as quantum support vector machines (QSVMs), quantum neural networks (QNNs), and quantum k-means clustering, have been developed to take advantage of the parallelism inherent in quantum computing. QSVMs, for instance, use quantum circuits to map data into a higher-dimensional space, making it easier to find a hyperplane that separates different classes. This quantum approach can potentially offer exponential speedups for certain types of classification problems.

Quantum neural networks, inspired by classical neural networks, consist of layers of quantum gates that process quantum data. These networks can exploit quantum entanglement and interference to capture complex patterns in data. Training a QNN involves adjusting the parameters of the quantum gates to minimize a loss function, a process that can be accelerated by quantum optimization algorithms. The potential of QNNs lies in their ability to model intricate relationships in data that are difficult for classical neural networks to capture.

Quantum k-means clustering, a quantum analog of the classical k-means algorithm, leverages quantum superposition to evaluate multiple cluster assignments simultaneously. By encoding data points into quantum states and using quantum distance measures, the algorithm can efficiently find the optimal clustering of data. This quantum approach can significantly reduce the time complexity of clustering large datasets, making it a valuable tool for data analysis.

A notable application of quantum machine learning is in the field of drug discovery. Traditional drug discovery methods involve screening vast libraries of compounds to identify potential drug candidates, a process that is both time-consuming and expensive. Quantum machine learning can accelerate this process by efficiently modeling molecular interactions and predicting the efficacy of compounds. For example, quantum versions of molecular docking algorithms can simulate the binding of drugs to target proteins more accurately and quickly than classical methods.

Another promising application is in finance. Quantum machine learning can enhance portfolio optimization, risk assessment, and fraud detection. In portfolio optimization, for instance, quantum algorithms can explore a vast number of possible asset allocations simultaneously, identifying the optimal portfolio that maximizes returns while minimizing risk. In fraud detection, quantum machine learning models can analyze complex transaction patterns to identify suspicious activities more effectively than classical models.

Despite the potential of quantum machine learning, several challenges remain. One of the primary challenges is the current state of quantum hardware. Quantum computers are still in their infancy, with limited qubits and high error rates. These limitations pose significant hurdles for implementing and scaling quantum machine learning algorithms. However, ongoing advancements in quantum hardware, such as error correction techniques and the development of more robust qubits, are gradually addressing these issues.

Another challenge is the need for hybrid quantum-classical approaches. Given the current limitations of quantum hardware, many quantum machine learning algorithms rely on classical preprocessing and postprocessing steps. These hybrid approaches combine the strengths of classical and quantum computing, allowing for practical implementations of quantum machine learning on near-term quantum devices. For example, a hybrid quantum-classical neural network might use a classical neural network for initial feature extraction, followed by a quantum neural network for final classification.

For beginners looking to explore quantum machine learning, a solid understanding of both quantum computing and classical machine learning is essential. Familiarity with quantum mechanics and quantum algorithms provides the foundation needed to grasp the principles of QML. Additionally, a strong background in classical machine learning helps in understanding how quantum techniques can be applied to traditional algorithms.

Practical experience with quantum programming is also crucial. Several quantum programming languages and frameworks, such as Qiskit, Cirq, and TensorFlow Quantum, offer tools for implementing quantum machine learning algorithms. These platforms provide simulators for testing quantum algorithms on classical hardware, as well as access to real quantum processors for running experiments. Engaging with these tools through hands-on projects and tutorials can accelerate the learning process.

Collaboration and community engagement are invaluable for advancing in the field of quantum machine learning. Joining online forums, attending workshops and conferences, and participating in collaborative research projects can provide insights, feedback, and support from other practitioners. The quantum computing community is rapidly growing, and being an active part of it can open up opportunities for learning and contribution.

Quantum machine learning is poised to transform various industries by offering novel solutions to complex problems. While the field is still in its early stages, the potential benefits are immense. As quantum hardware continues to evolve and mature, the capabilities of quantum machine learning will expand, bringing us closer to realizing its full potential. By building a strong foundation in both quantum computing and classical machine learning, staying engaged with the community, and embracing hybrid approaches, beginners can position themselves at the forefront of this exciting and rapidly advancing field.

In summary, quantum machine learning represents a frontier of technological innovation, merging the principles of quantum mechanics with the power of machine learning. Through quantum data encoding, the application of quantum algorithms, and the exploration of practical applications, QML offers unprecedented opportunities for solving complex problems. Despite current challenges, the ongoing advancements in quantum hardware and the collaborative efforts of the quantum computing community are paving the way for a future where quantum machine learning becomes a transformative force across various domains.

Emerging Applications and Use Cases

Emerging applications and use cases of quantum computing offer a glimpse into a future where the boundaries of current technology are pushed far beyond their present limits. Quantum computing, with its potential to solve problems exponentially faster than classical computers, is poised to revolutionize multiple industries. This chapter delves into some of the most promising applications and use cases that are beginning to take shape, illustrating the transformative potential of this cutting-edge technology.

One of the most anticipated applications of quantum computing is in the field of cryptography. Traditional cryptographic methods rely on the difficulty of factoring large numbers, a task that classical computers find exceedingly time-consuming as the numbers grow larger. Quantum computers, however, can employ Shor's algorithm to factor these numbers exponentially faster, rendering many current encryption schemes vulnerable. This potential has spurred the development of quantum-resistant cryptographic algorithms, ensuring the security of sensitive information in a post-quantum world. Governments and organizations are investing heavily in quantum-safe encryption methods to prepare for the inevitable advancements in quantum computing capabilities.

In the realm of pharmaceuticals and healthcare, quantum computing promises to accelerate drug discovery and development. Classical methods of drug discovery involve simulating molecular interactions, a process that becomes increasingly complex with larger molecules. Quantum computers can simulate these interactions more accurately and efficiently, potentially identifying new drug candidates in a fraction of the time. For example, researchers are exploring the use of quantum computing to simulate the behavior of proteins, understanding their folding patterns, and designing drugs that can effectively target specific diseases. This capability could lead to breakthroughs in treating conditions that currently have limited therapeutic options.

Another exciting application of quantum computing lies in optimizing supply chains and logistics. Classical optimization algorithms often struggle with the sheer complexity of global supply chains, where numerous variables and constraints must be considered simultaneously. Quantum optimization algorithms can evaluate many potential solutions at once, identifying the most efficient routes and schedules for transporting goods. Companies like Volkswagen have already begun experimenting with quantum algorithms to optimize traffic flow in urban environments, reducing congestion and improving overall efficiency. As quantum hardware continues to advance, these optimization capabilities will become increasingly accessible and impactful.

Finance is another sector poised to benefit significantly from quantum computing. Financial institutions deal with vast amounts of data and complex models to manage risk, optimize portfolios, and execute high-frequency trading strategies. Quantum computing can process and analyze this data more rapidly, providing more accurate risk assessments and enabling better decision-making. For instance, quantum algorithms can be used to model and predict market behavior, helping traders to develop more effective strategies. Additionally, quantum computing can enhance fraud detection by identifying subtle patterns and anomalies in transaction data that classical algorithms might miss.

Quantum computing also holds promise for advancing artificial intelligence and machine learning. Quantum machine learning algorithms can process and analyze large datasets more efficiently than classical algorithms, potentially leading to significant improvements in pattern recognition, natural language processing, and image analysis. Researchers are exploring quantum neural networks, which mimic the structure and function of classical neural networks but leverage quantum properties to perform computations. These networks could revolutionize fields such as autonomous driving, where rapid and accurate data processing is crucial for safety and performance.

In the field of materials science, quantum computing offers the ability to simulate and design new materials with unprecedented precision. Understanding the properties of materials at the quantum level allows scientists to predict how they will behave under different conditions. This capability can lead to the development of materials with novel properties, such as superconductors that operate at higher temperatures or more efficient photovoltaic cells for solar energy. By simulating material behavior at the atomic level, quantum computers can accelerate the discovery and optimization of materials for a wide range of applications.

Climate modeling and environmental science are other areas where quantum computing can make a substantial impact. Accurate climate models are essential for understanding and mitigating the effects of climate change, but these models require immense computational resources. Quantum computers can handle the complex calculations involved in climate modeling more efficiently, providing more accurate predictions and insights. For example, quantum simulations can help researchers understand the interactions between various components of the Earth's climate system, leading to better strategies for reducing greenhouse gas emissions and mitigating climate impacts.

The entertainment industry is also beginning to explore the potential of quantum computing. Quantum algorithms can be used to create more realistic simulations and special effects in movies and video games. By processing vast amounts of data related to physics and human behavior, quantum computers can generate more lifelike animations and environments. Additionally, quantum computing can enhance virtual reality experiences by improving the rendering and interaction of complex virtual worlds. As the technology matures, we can expect quantum computing to play a significant role in creating more immersive and engaging entertainment experiences.

Despite the tremendous potential of quantum computing, there are still several challenges to overcome before these applications become mainstream. One of the primary challenges is the development of stable and scalable quantum hardware. Current quantum computers are prone to errors and have limited qubit counts, which restrict their ability to solve large-scale problems. Advances in quantum error correction and the development of more robust qubits are essential for realizing the full potential of quantum computing.

Another challenge is the need for specialized expertise and resources to develop and implement quantum algorithms. Quantum computing requires a deep understanding of quantum mechanics, computer science, and specific domain knowledge relevant to the application. Building interdisciplinary teams that can bridge these knowledge gaps is crucial for successful quantum computing projects. Additionally, developing user-friendly tools and frameworks for quantum programming will help democratize access to quantum computing capabilities.

Regulatory and ethical considerations also play a significant role in the adoption of quantum computing. As with any powerful technology, it is essential to ensure that quantum computing is used responsibly and ethically. This includes addressing concerns related to data privacy, security, and the potential societal impacts of quantum computing. Establishing clear guidelines and standards for the use of quantum technology will help mitigate risks and promote its beneficial applications.

The journey of quantum computing from theoretical research to practical applications is still in its early stages, but the progress made so far is promising. As quantum hardware continues to advance and more researchers and organizations explore its potential, we can expect to see an increasing number of innovative and impactful use cases. Quantum computing has the potential to transform industries, solve complex problems, and drive technological advancements that were previously unimaginable.

In conclusion, emerging applications and use cases of quantum computing highlight its transformative potential across various fields. From cryptography and drug discovery to supply chain optimization and climate modeling, quantum computing offers unprecedented capabilities for solving complex problems. While challenges remain, ongoing advancements in quantum hardware, interdisciplinary collaboration, and responsible use will pave the way for a future where quantum computing revolutionizes technology and industry. By staying informed and engaged with the latest developments, we can prepare for the exciting possibilities that quantum computing holds.